GOLDEN ARMS
aka Test Pilots

GOLDEN ARMS
aka Test Pilots

SIX YEARS THAT CHANGED AERIAL WARFARE

Michael Williams with Lance Grace

SUNSTONE PRESS
SANTA FE

≈≈≈

© 2017 by Michael Williams with Lance Grace
All Rights Reserved.

No part of this book may be reproduced in any form or by any electronic or mechanical means including information storage and retrieval systems without permission in writing from the publisher, except by a reviewer who may quote brief passages in a review.

Sunstone books may be purchased for educational, business, or sales promotional use.
For information please write: Special Markets Department, Sunstone Press,
P.O. Box 2321, Santa Fe, New Mexico 87504-2321.

Body typeface › Minion Pro
Printed on acid-free paper
∞

Library of Congress Cataloging-in-Publication Data
Names: Williams, Michael, 1958 Aug. 20- author. | Grace, Lance C., 1952- author.
Title: Golden arms, aka test pilot : six years that changed aerial warfare / by Michael Williams with Lance C. Grace ; photography by Michael Williams.
Description: Santa Fe : Sunstone Press, [2017]
Identifiers: LCCN 2016046447 | ISBN 9781632931610 (softcover : alk. paper) ISBN 9781632932075 (hardcover : akl. paper)
Subjects: LCSH: Airplanes, Military--United States--History--20th century--Pictorial works. | Research aircraft--United States--History--20th century--Pictorial works. | White Sands Missile Range (N.M.)--History--Pictorial works. | United States. Air Force. Flight Test Squadron, 568th--History--Pictorial works. | Test pilots--United States--Biography. | Proving grounds--New Mexico--History--20th century--Pictorial works.
Classification: LCC UG1240 .W52 2017 | DDC 358.4/07--dc23
LC record available at https://lccn.loc.gov/2016046447

SUNSTONE PRESS IS COMMITTED TO MINIMIZING OUR ENVIRONMENTAL IMPACT ON THE PLANET. THE PAPER USED IN THIS BOOK IS FROM RESPONSIBLY MANAGED FORESTS. OUR PRINTER HAS RECEIVED CHAIN OF CUSTODY (COC) CERTIFICATION FROM: THE FOREST STEWARDSHIP COUNCIL™ (FSC®), PROGRAMME FOR THE ENDORSEMENT OF FOREST CERTIFICATION™ (PEFC™), AND THE SUSTAINABLE FORESTRY INITIATIVE® (SFI®). THE FSC® COUNCIL IS A NON-PROFIT ORGANIZATION, PROMOTING THE ENVIRONMENTALLY APPROPRIATE, SOCIALLY BENEFICIAL AND ECONOMICALLY VIABLE MANAGEMENT OF THE WORLD'S FORESTS. FSC® CERTIFICATION IS RECOGNIZED INTERNATIONALLY AS A RIGOROUS ENVIRONMENTAL AND SOCIAL STANDARD FOR RESPONSIBLE FOREST MANAGEMENT.

WWW.SUNSTONEPRESS.COM
SUNSTONE PRESS / POST OFFICE BOX 2321 / SANTA FE, NM 87504-2321 /USA
(505) 988-4418 / ORDERS ONLY (800) 243-5644 / FAX (505) 988-1025

Photography by
Michael Williams

"Mike's book brings back to life missions that took place during my tenure as the Commander of the 586th Flight Test Squadron, as well as the most beautiful! Each photo brings back vivid memories and a multitude of stories stemming from a vast variety of test programs that the squadron accomplished during those years. Some of the programs had far reaching and dramatic effects on the USAF, the US military, and aviation. Each squadron member can be proud of the vital role that each had played to make it happen."

—Lance C. Grace, Lieutenant Colonel (Retired), USAF

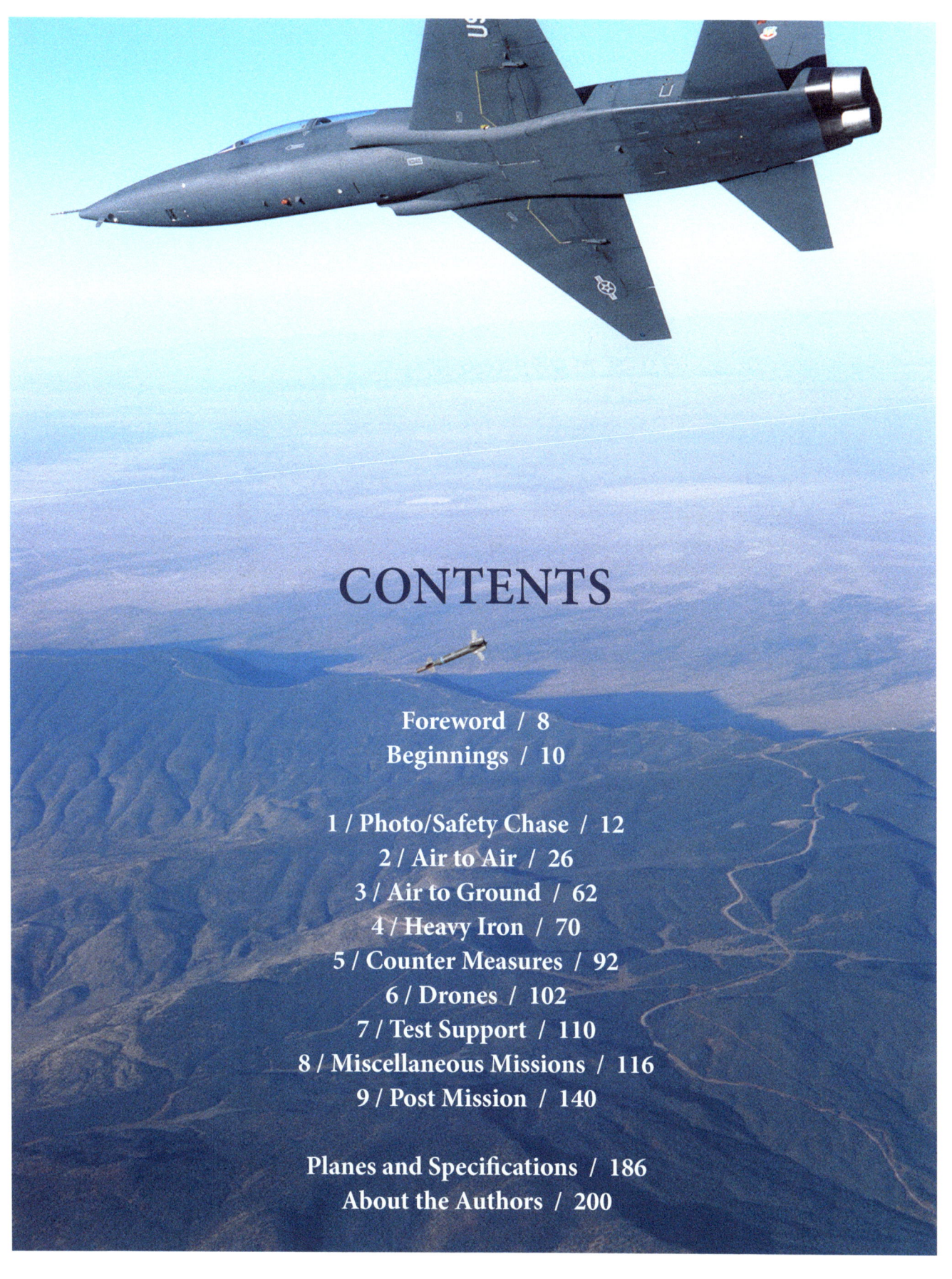

CONTENTS

Foreword / 8
Beginnings / 10

1 / Photo/Safety Chase / 12
2 / Air to Air / 26
3 / Air to Ground / 62
4 / Heavy Iron / 70
5 / Counter Measures / 92
6 / Drones / 102
7 / Test Support / 110
8 / Miscellaneous Missions / 116
9 / Post Mission / 140

Planes and Specifications / 186
About the Authors / 200

FOREWORD

For most, it's difficult to fathom the enormous challenges and calculated risks embraced by the men and women who work so tirelessly to push the envelope in military aviation. As a test pilot who flew the most advanced fighters in our nation's arsenal today, I'm often asked what it feels like to fly faster than the speed of sound or to deploy a live missile. Mike Williams offers an exquisite behind-the-scenes look at the challenge and thrill associated with flying at the edge of the envelope and beyond.

Mike takes the reader back to a time when the nation's airpower development program focused on improving an aircraft's combat capability through a variety of missions: faster missiles, larger and more accurate bombs and systems designed to improve targeting accuracy and a pilot's situational awareness. The importance of documenting such missions—some, one-of-a-kind and many costing in the multi-million-dollar range—at the most critical juncture during the test was essential. The pressure on a chase pilot and the aerial photographer in his backseat to capture useable photographic evidence was immense and not for the faint of heart.

Great aerial photographers are true artists. I feel fortunate to have flown with the best, Mike included. And although test engineers were delighted to see visual confirmation of the data they required upon completion of a chase mission, I was afforded a different point of view from the one I had just experienced flying the plane. In reviewing photographs taken from my back seat or from the chase plane alongside me, I marveled at how a talented eye could capture not only the necessary data points, but also the beauty and majesty of those airborne moments.

Beyond the artistry was a true bond formed between chase pilot and photographer—we were in it together! A strong fiber of trust and friendship forms quickly when a plane's nose is pointed straight down at speeds of 1.4Mach.

Mike's gorgeous photographs and stories will take you there, recreating that rush, that edge-of-your-seat appreciation for an art form born out of trust and respect.

—Lieutenant Colonel Paul "TP" Smith, USAF, Ret.,
Director and Chief Test Pilot,
Joint Strike Fighter (X-35) Test Program

BEGINNINGS

Having enlisted into the United States Air Force in 1977, I became a Defensive Fire Control Mechanic on B-52G aircraft. Working on the flight line, a few yards from the runway, I would notice T-38's practicing touch-and-go landings. I was fascinated how the T-38 would take-off and skid across the sky as it climbed, thinking what a great job that would be. A few years later, I had the opportunity to cross-train into motion picture photography. My first assignment as a photographer was at Hill AFB supporting munitions life-cycle testing. This allowed me to fly in O-2, H-53, and C-130 aircraft supporting cruise missile launch and profile tests. But I never got the opportunity to fly in fast-movers that supported other types of tests being conducted.

Afterwards, I was assigned to Hickam AFB to support the Pacific's Falling Star program. This now declassified program retrieved film capsules from overhead satellites during the Cold War. After the last satellites were destroyed during the Challenger mishap and subsequent Titan Rocket launch failure, the program folded.

Our unit quickly transitioned into Video Documentation, providing video and historical documentation to different activities and events throughout the Pacific. During this tour, I learned to shoot and edit a story aesthetically.

Next came an assignment that I had waited for my entire career. It was at Holloman AFB, New Mexico, a one deep position that supported flight testing over White Sands Missile Range (WSMR) flying T-38's and F-15 aircraft.

Having been exposed to flight testing at Hill, I thought if I'd ever have an opportunity to fly fast movers, I would try and combine optical instrumentation needed for research and development with photographic artistry, creating scientific, but aesthetically pleasing pictures. But I needed a way to accomplish this.

I had the good fortune of my predecessor acquiring a unique camera set-up that combined a high-speed motion picture camera with a sequential still camera. This eventually allowed us to do what no other photo chase in the world could accomplish, acquiring three formats, still, motion picture, and video from a single aircraft. I now had the capability to do what I wanted; all I needed to do was put my plan into action.

My job was to go up and chase aircraft, firing the world's most lethal missiles. This required lightening quick reflexes during events lasting only three seconds. This was the easy part. The hard part was getting over airsickness.

My chase pilot would always get me where I needed to be, when I needed to be there. He would also go out of his way after the event to get me sick. I measured my progress the first year by how close I could get back to the airfield without vomiting. Eventually it made me bullet proof, enhancing my situational awareness during missions.

Later, I was aircrew certified to fly in three fast movers, the T-38, F-15, and F16, a rarity within Material Command. This gave me the opportunity to fly and participate in the top tests being conducted in the Department of Defense, acquiring the pictures this book is compiled with. I honestly believe there is no other collection anywhere in the world containing flight test photography of this caliber for you to witness and enjoy.

1 PHOTO/SAFETY CHASE

This is what it was all about; to ensure tests were conducted in a safe and controlled manner while documenting weapons coming off airplanes. Although these test scenarios went very fast, what led up to them was very fascinating.

First, the aircraft we used were mismatched in both power and maneuverability. F-15 and F-16 fighters were flown as test platforms, but for economy, T-38 trainers were used as chase. What the T-38 lacked in performance, they compensated by having distortion free canopies, essential for aerial photography

Second, tests conducted at the White Sands Missile Range were always over land. This meant test controllers positioned the drone, test, and chase aircraft into the shot box at the same time. The shot box ensured the drone or stray missile would go down in a controlled area. With each aircraft having different flying characteristics, this was never an easy task.

With these factors in mind, choreography became very important. It was well planned and rehearsed prior to the actual test or "hot" mission. During the test, the chase aircraft was a secondary player. How close we got in, depended on how important the event was. Sometimes you had to be very close to observe a critical function. Other times, you could be positioned a mile away. But when the mission called for photo chase, we were always within 50 to 100 feet of the action.

So, how do you stay with an aircraft with a plane that doesn't have the performance of a fighter? You may say the pilot in the other plane just has to be nice and give you some latitude. Of course, it doesn't work that way. He had too many things going on. So as chase, you had to have a plan.

Our plan was to keep altitude, saving potential energy in order to trade it for kinetic at the appropriate time. When we started the chase, we would be ten miles out from the firing or "fox" point, staying 10,000 feet above the shooter. As the shooter lit his afterburners, we lit ours, eliminating all of the induced drag, and ramping down in altitude.

Once we got alongside the airplane, we put the engine to idle and deployed our boards (speed brakes). Then it was full left aileron, full right rudder, putting out as much drag as possible to bleed-off speed to avoid passing the shooters 3/9 (wing) line.

Using this technique, we would get into position two to three seconds prior to the missile being launched. Although it looks like a nice static shot, what led up to it was unbelievably aggressive.

CHASE PILOT

CHASE PILOT

It is amazing what you can do with a thirty-year old T-38. Coming into flight test and Air Force Material Command (AFMC) from Air Education and Training Command (AETC) was a real learning experience. AETC is very conservative, sometimes excessively so due to the fact that the command's mission is to train new Air Force pilots. With that in mind, AETC must instill a "straight arrow" attitude into student pilots. Only after students move to their operational commands are they allowed to decide which habits and procedures are valid, and which ones should be given up to individual judgment. Thus, AETC writes its flight regulations accordingly.

AFMC is different (put mildly). Almost all of its pilots are extremely experienced, having hundreds, and sometimes thousands of hours in a particular aircraft. AFMC doesn't have to regulate judgment; flying regulations are the minimum necessary to accomplish the mission. Without this latitude, test pilots would not be able to fly at the level necessary to reach test points or achieve particular test parameters.

So, what does all this have to do with the T-38? Well, while chasing different air-to-air and air-to-ground weapons, I got to fly faster (1.4 Mach), higher (49,000 feet), and slower (140 knots outside the traffic pattern) in a T-38 than I would have, if I had been assigned to AETC!

The 1.4 Mach flight was very interesting. Mike and I were chasing a GBU-28 "Bunker Buster" bomb. This 5,000 pound weapon manufactured from a howitzer barrel was made famous during Desert Storm for its unbelievable penetration abilities. On this test, the bomb was dropped from an F-111 flying at 40,000 feet. We were there to capture the safe separation of the bomb from the aircraft, as well as the deployment of the tail fins necessary to guide the weapon into the target (bunker).

A side objective (as always) was to track the weapon for as long as possible, hopefully into the target. As the weapon released, we went to idle power and deployed the speed brakes to emulate the bomb's drag characteristics. Tracking a gravity weapon (with a photographer and fifteen pounds of camera equipment) can be a dicey task. We spiraled around the bomb as it tipped over into vertical as I tried to minimize the g-load to prevent the camera being forced into Mike's lap.

The bomb continued to fall, well, like a bomb, as we stayed aft and paralleled to its flight path. As this was occurring, I happened to glance into the cockpit and noticed 1.4 Mach on the airspeed gauge. Passing through 15,000 feet, I began the dive recovery, while trying to minimize the g's for Mike, but he hung tough as his fifteen pound camera suddenly weighed near 80 pounds. By the way, we tracked the weapon all the way into its target.

Anyone who has flown the T-38 knows that it likes to go fast at attitudes above 35,000 feet. Unfortunately, its level acceleration capabilities are somewhat limited, so when we chased other aircraft having more power and greater acceleration, we needed to "ramp down" from altitude to catch the "event" by being in position, on speed, just prior to launch.

Chasing an F-15 flying 1.2 Mach at 39,000 feet definitely requires such a maneuver, so we climbed the T-38 to 49,000 feet in max afterburner and leveled out as close to 1.0 Mach as possible. Prior to the "event", we began our max afterburner descent to catch the F-15. Passing through 47,000 feet, our left engine fire light illuminated. Arbitrarily throwing the throttle to idle at that altitude could cause the aft end of the aircraft to depart, taking the engine with it, I decided to act with caution and check my engine instruments for other signs of a fire. No such luck, in the two seconds it took to scan my engine instruments (with no indication of a problem), the fire light went out. Was this some sort of "high altitude/high Mach" problem? Who knows, we "knocked off" the pass and returned home. Of course, maintenance could find nothing wrong with the aircraft.

By far, one of the most interesting chase missions we flew was also one of the most challenging. We were contacted by NASA to provide photo chase support of the DC-X "Delta Clipper" single-stage-to-orbit vehicle during its flight profile from White Sands Missile Range.

The DC-X prototype vehicle was designed as a technological demonstrator for an inexpensive, reusable way to deliver objects into orbit on a smaller scale than the Space Shuttle. Apollo 12 mission commander, Mr. Charles "Pete" Conrad was in charge of the flight.

The DC-X profile, which was the most complex up to that time, was to take off vertically, climb to 9,000 feet, translate horizontally about a mile, pitch from vertical to ten degrees nose low, pitch back to vertical, and return to its original launch point for a vertical landing.

We chased this "rocket", at least it flew like a rocket, with an F-15D and AT-38 to cover both its launch/landing (low altitude) and mid-profile flight (high altitude). Timing, speed, and turn radius was critical, as we wanted to fly no closer or further than 2000 feet to the DC-X in case it exploded in flight.

T-38's are not well known for their turning performance, so we got into the charts and found that the best technique would be to fly at approximately 220 knots with flaps set at 40 percent for additional lift. The actual flight went flawlessly, with the F-15D and AT-38 holding well clear of the launch pad until lift-off. Unfortunately our hold point proved to be right over the VIP observation area, giving guests an unintentional airshow.

23

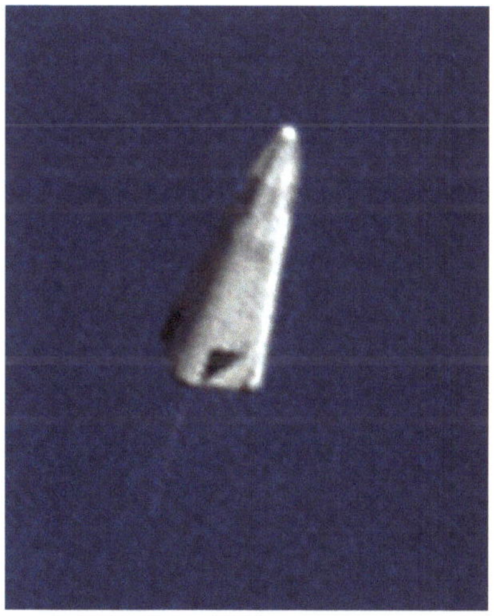

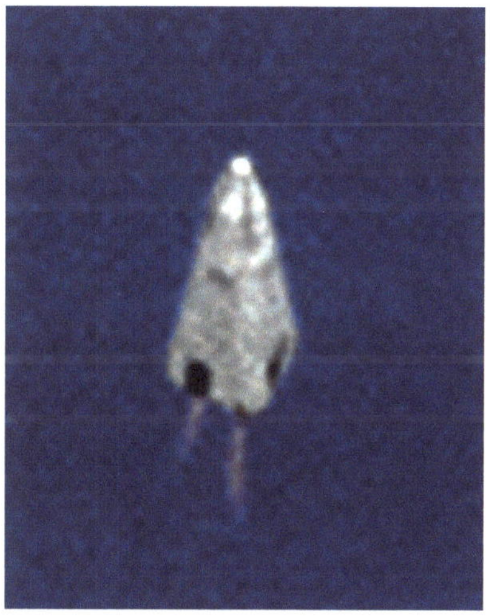

On lift-off, our aircraft were in position on opposite sides of the 2,000 foot circle. I covered the launch from a position about 500 feet above ground level, with the F-15D stacking higher to cover the climb and tip-over positions of the flight profile. Boy! It was quite a task to keep my helmet mounted camera centered on the DC-X, while pulling as many g's as we possibly could. I didn't envy the photographers as they tried to do the same thing with heavy camera equipment.

On descent, we found ourselves fairly nose low (about 40 degrees) trying to beat the DC-X down to film its landing. The recovery was pretty abrupt, however, "we got the shot" and filmed the landing of a very successful flight.

Yeah, T-38's are old and underpowered, but they make a pretty good chase plane.

—Major Dave "Big Wave" Burke, USAF, Ret.

2 AIR TO AIR

WSEP

This is the first shot I ever took over the range. It's an AIM-7 Sparrow radar guided missile launched by an F-15A for the Weapons System Evaluation Program (WSEP), a program to allow pilots to fire a missile at least once in their career.

Notice the smoke coming out of the rear. If the pilot missed its target, the smoke trail would lead his adversary back to him. This necessitated a change in our tactics.

Engineers worked on this issue during the late 1980's and early 1990's. What they came up with was, the Advanced Medium Range Air-to-Air Missile or AMRAAM. Besides a smokeless exhaust, they gave it more power, a longer range, and shoot and forget capabilities.

F-16 AIR DEFENSE FIGHTER

The F-16 Air Defense Fighter (ADF) flew to Holloman from Edwards AFB to fire this AIM-7 missile. Although the F-16 was an all-weather fighter, its weapon systems weren't. The F-16 was designed for guns and heat seeking missiles, which both could be defeated by cloud cover. In fact, the Air Force called the F-16 a clear air-mass fighter. This remained true until the early 90's.

For the test, an F-16A was modified, so it could compete in a fly-off against the F-4 and F-20 to see which fighter could step into the interceptor role vacated by the retiring F-106 Delta Dart. To do this, program managers needed an all-weather missile. Engineers decided on the AIM-7, stuck it on the airframe, and integrated the missile with the F-16's radar system, which was quite a feat in itself.

So, this is the shot, the first AIM-7 missile to be fired from an F-16. It was done from Holloman AFB and over the White Sands Missile Range.

F-15E AMRAAM

On the wing of this F-15E, you can see a number of weapons. The missile mounted on the bottom is a captive carry Advanced Medium Range Air-Air Missile (AMRAAM) used for testing. It allows a pilot to simulate launching a missile prior to launching the test item. Above it, is a B-61 nuclear bomb. It's not really a "nuke," but a test pod with all the components of the bomb except the warhead itself. On top is the "live" AMRAAM that would be used for the test.

AIM-120 AMRAAM MISSILE INFLIGHT

The AIM-120 AMRAAM missile is ten feet long, eight inches thick, and rocket propelled. You can distinguish AMRAAM inflight from the AIM-7 Sparrow by its smaller canards and smokeless trail.

FIRST F-15E AMRAAM LAUNCH

The first AMRAAM launch off an F-15E was interesting because it shows why you have tests, and why you use photography. To integrate the weapon to the airframe, program engineers installed a computer having high-speed integrated chips. In the process, they inadvertently reprogrammed the software. After the computer was installed, program engineers felt it wasn't necessary to test the system, since only the hardware was modified and not the software.

A test engineer at Holloman associated with the program didn't agree, and forced the others to fire the missile. So they came to Holloman and took the shot. The interesting thing was, the missile came off and launched into the ground. Out of seventy-two AMRAAM missions, this was the first failure that we had ever encountered.

After the sortie, we reviewed the footage from the chase pilot's helmet cam. The footage showed that the missile went out, straightened, and then dove down. Our first thought was, "Boy, the missile lofted into the ground!" I mean, AMRAAM normally lofts-up after launch. They come off, decide where the target is, build-up energy and pitch-up. In this case, it went out and pitched down.

To us, it looked like it lofted into the dirt, and sure enough, that's exactly what happened. A coordinated transfer problem was induced during the software change. Somebody put in a minus instead of a plus. So, the missile went out, looked at the target, figured out what was going on, and decided, yes, I need to loft, but had its directions 180 degrees backwards and went into the dirt.

F-15E SEQUENCE

Even though the following sequence looks perfect, the missile shot was a failure. Engineers were able to identify the problem by reviewing the test footage right after we landed. These pictures were taken with a 70mm sequential camera at 10 frames per second.

AMRAAM TEST PLATFORMS

These were the launch platforms AMRAAM was designed for. The top picture shows tail number 045, the primary Air Force F-15 test aircraft for AMRAAM. In the center, is an Operational Test F-16C that shot down several drones during test evaluations conducted over WSMR. Below is a Naval Air Weapons Center F-18 that also ventured out to the range to test the weapon.

MISSILE IMPACT

This shows what happened often during missions. Most of the time, we fired missiles without warheads. This meant missiles had to impact the drone in order to take them out.

As the missile impacts the aircraft, it goes through the fuselage, damaging the aircraft's structural integrity. As the aircraft spins, aerodynamic forces are exerted on the drone, ripping it apart as it explodes.

AIM-9X

BOX-OFFICE AIM-9X

We were involved with the development of this missile for many years. It's called the AIM-9X Box-Office missile, the compressed variant of the AIM-9 Sidewinder. It was created for the new F-22 and F-35 aircraft during the 1980's and 1990's. Prior to air launching a new missile, it has to go through numerous ground and airborne testing. The picture on the right shows the missile's configuration for shake, rattle, and roll testing to see if the internal construction can withstand both positive and negative g-loads. The AIM-9X had to be compressed smaller than the AIM-9 missile that it replaces, since all the missile racks on the new fighters were supposed to be internally stored.

By contrasting the missile that was fired to the AIM-9 on the outboard wing, you can see the differences in size and shape. Most of the external flight control surfaces have been removed, and have been augmented with flight vectoring control vanes mounted in the rocket's exhaust port, giving it authoritative thrust.

To evaluate its launch characteristics, you have to compare how different missiles initiate. For example, the AIM-7 ejects off the fuselage of the F-15, dropping ten feet into the airstream before the engine ignites. Once lit, the missile builds-up momentum very quickly. AMRAAM on the other hand, can either be ejected off the fuselage, or rail launched to come off even quicker.

When you get to heat seeking missiles, they are like a pop-bottle rocket. When you take a shot, everything is already decided. The missile zips off the rail and it's gone.

Now, let's say you have a pop-bottle rocket and put some extra oomph on it. That's what this missile was all about. When it came off, it was away. The photographer had to pan the camera at the exact moment, or he'd miss the shot. Timing was everything. We had to rehearse these missions more than any test we ever did. It would come down to the shooter saying, "Ready, Ready, Fox," meaning missile away, whoosh, and the missile was gone, all in the blink of an eye.

What else is special about the AIM-9X, is the helmet mounted cueing system that allows the pilot to slave the missile towards any target within 170 degrees, meaning he can shoot down an aircraft that's behind him without ever having to point the aircraft towards it.

AIM-9X LAUNCH SEQUENCE

The AIM-9X has unbelievable maneuvering capabilities. It can be shot while the aircraft is under an incredible amount of g's. In this sequence, the F-16 is in an "S" turn to the right. The drone is close-by and to the left. An impossible shot right? The missile has to come off, turn in the opposite direction of travel, and goes after the target. It's tough, but it can be done.

AIM-9X CLOSE-UP

The AIM-9 mounted on the wing tip is actually an AIM-9 shell used as a camera pod. Within it, are two 16mm cameras linked to the trigger. This allows the cameras to start at the same time the pilot launches the missile. The high speed cameras ran at 200 frames per second to document missile separation. Later, the slow motion footage would be analyzed by engineers for discrepancies.

HAVE DASH II

HAVE DASH II

Have Dash II was a follow-on demonstration program that used advanced airframes for air-to-air missiles. The concept was to make missiles fly more like airplanes. Most conventional missiles use forward flight controls with an X configuration. When a missile is launched, it maintains this profile by aligning itself with the ground. If the missile needs to change direction, it skids into the turn, keeping the X configuration to the ground. It works, but it's not as efficient as if the flight controls were in a plus configuration allowing the missile to roll into a turn like a plane.

Have Dash II was designed with this in mind, allowing it to maneuver more efficiently, maintain more energy and travel greater distances, all because it could turn like a plane. Although it was powered by an AIM-7 rocket motor, the intention was to develop a rocket and air breathing hybrid engine to give it greater range and hypersonic speeds. Although it flew pre-programmed flight profiles that included banks and turns achieving 50 g's, it was never launched at a moving target

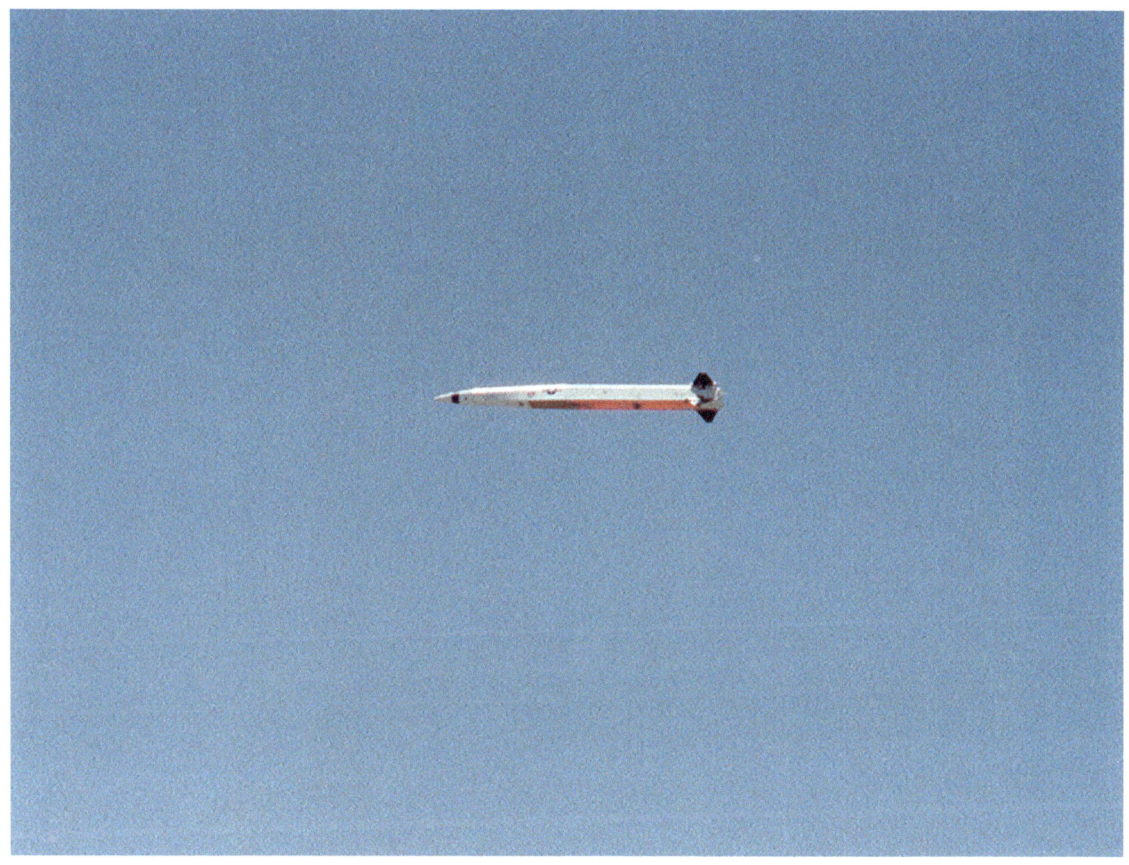

HAVE DASH II CLOSE-UP

Mounted on the F-16's wing, is the Have Dash II missile. The rear wings were folded prior to launch for a couple of reasons. One was to improve its stealth characteristics by reducing the missile's radar reflecting surfaces. The other was to increase load capacities inside internal weapon bays for future aircraft, such as the F-22.

Another interesting thing about these wings were, they required thermal batteries to generate the electricity to open-up and go through a pre-programmed check-out sequence. The only way to verify that this procedure actually happened was for the chase to get in close and observe them open into position. We would inch our way in until we were a couple of feet away, watch the wings lock-in, then drop 100 feet into chase position to document the launch. If everything worked correctly, it would take us about 10 seconds from check-out to documenting the launch.

3 AIR TO GROUND

STAND OFF LAND ATTACK MISSILE (SLAM)

We did tests for other services too. This Navy A-6 is launching the first Global Positioning System (GPS) assisted AGM-84 Harpoon Stand-Off Attack Missile (SLAM). In 1989, only twelve of the system's twenty seven satellites were orbiting the earth. Because of this, the test had to be planned when we had the correct number of satellites overhead, which happened to be 5:30 in the morning. This was the second earliest shot I ever took. The earliest was a video shoot at 3:30 a.m. catching an EC-130 light-up the sky dispensing flares over the White Sands.

    Having a 60 mile range, the Harpoon missile was one of two missiles that we could fly in formation with, the other being the Tomahawk. As you can see, early morning shots in New Mexico also produce the most colorful backdrops that you can imagine.

HAVE-NAP

AGM-142 HAVE NAP AIR-TO-SURFACE MISSILE

Having a 60 mile range, the Israeli made AGM-142 Have Nap air-to-surface missile is launched from a B-52H bomber. On the nose of the missile, an assortment of optical or imaging infrared sensors can be installed, providing a visual data link back to the bombardier who guides the missile to the designated target. It was not unusual during these tests to hear the bombardier say, "Which window do you want it in, left or right?" That is how accurate these systems are.

Have Nap contains a solid rocket booster. As the missile drops off the airplane, the rocket motor ignites, and "boosts" the missile down range as it climbs in altitude before the air-breathing engine initiates.

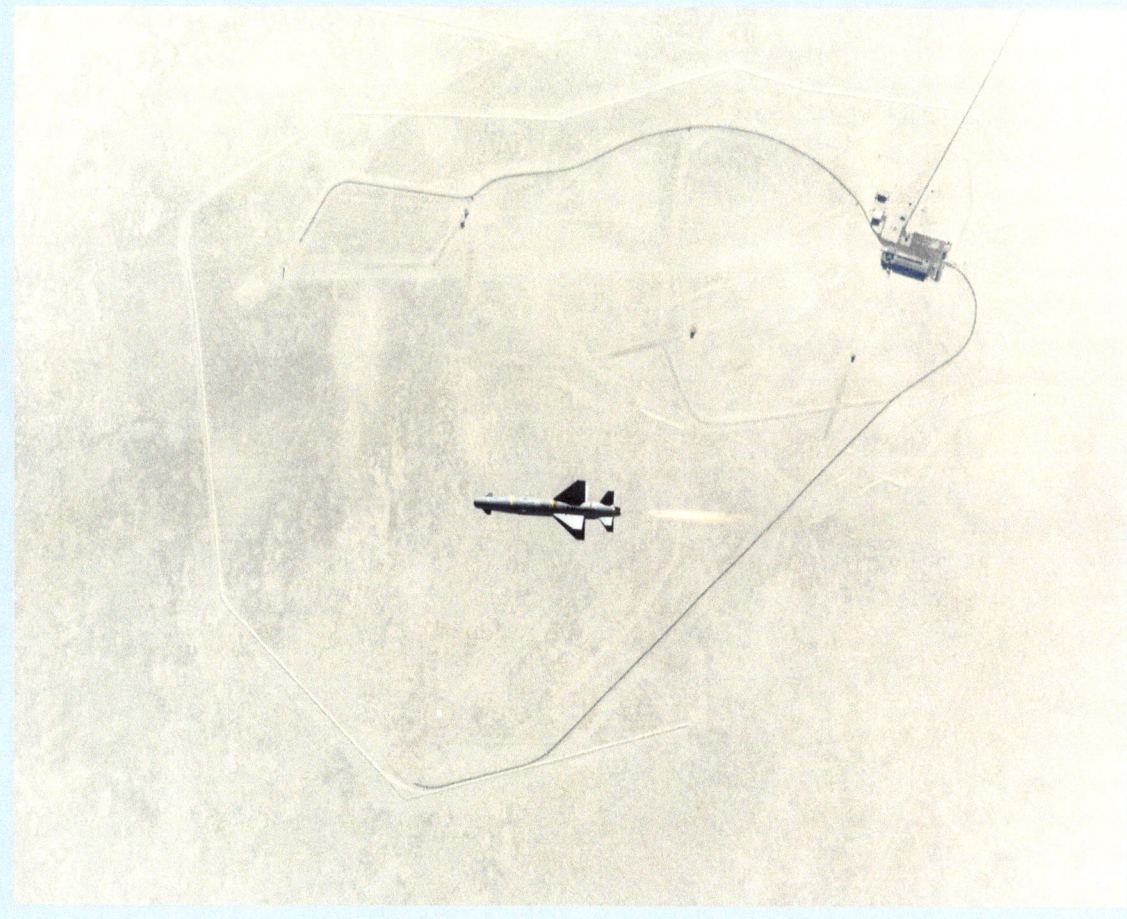

Here, a B-52H from Barksdale AFB flies by "Toby Town," the designated impact zone for Have Nap missile tests on White Sands Missile Range. The bunker in the upper right corner of the compound was the target for that day's test.

4 HEAVY IRON

THUNDERBIRD AVIATION'S F-8

Sometimes, we supported private contractors who flew for the government. One such contractor was Thunderbird Aviation. At the time, Thunderbird had a small Air Force consisting of a C-123 Caribou, an A-3 "Whale," a T-33, seven A-7's, and a couple of F-8's. The F-8 Crusader you see here was the last one flying in North America. During this flight, it was dropping the cluster bomb that can be seen under the wing. Although they had on-board cameras catching the separation, they needed a safety chase to conduct the test.

GBU-28

The GBU-28 bunker-busting bomb made for Saddam during DESERT STORM was created in 17 days. It is 27 feet long, weighs 5,000 pounds, and was dropped from either the F-15E or the FB-111 aircraft. I did several of these test missions, including a record setting drop of over 40,000 feet that came within 3 feet of its target.

I flew with the pilot who dropped the first one the day prior to the event. The call came while we were still up in the air, telling him that he would have a classified project the next day. The next morning, he flew over to Nellis AFB and dropped the bomb.

After the drop, engineers started digging immediately after it impacted the ground. They gave up after 100 feet. The next day the bomb was on its way to Iraq.

DETACHMENT 1, 57TH FIGHTER WING DRAGON TEAM

Major Paul Dolson oversaw the 57th Fighter Wing's Dragon Team operations at Holloman AFB. They were detached from Nellis AFB to enhance the capabilities of the Stealth Fighter. Not really a fighter, the F-117 was a small scale bomber that could hold two, two thousand pound GBU-27 bombs, or other ordinances in its bomb bay.

Lacking photographic support, Paul wondered if he could "borrow me" on occasion to document tests they were conducting. One such test was called, the consecutive miracle shot. The story he told me, was, during a discussion, pilots and engineers were trying to figure out how two, two thousand pound bombs carried by the F-117 could penetrate a reinforced bomb shelter buried out in the desert. After several minutes, a janitor who was cleaning inside the room spoke-up, saying, "Why don't you drop one after the other?" Everyone in the room looked-up and said, "Hmm!"

Later, engineers found that if you dropped a second bomb within a few hundredths-of-a-second of the first, the first bomb would crack the shelter, and the second one would break through. This meant pinpoint accuracy from thousands of feet away. You have to remember that during World War II, it took close to two hundred missions to take out one target. Now, it's one for one, ouala, the consecutive miracle shot, and here it is.

F-117 OVER ELEPHANT BUTTE AND GBU-27 DROP SEQUENCE

I would fly many sorties with Paul and the unit's other pilot, Major Dan DeCamp. I was invited to fly with them whenever they were flying T-38's, since they had no one else to fly in the back seat. Several times I would go out and fly with Dan and we would just alternate flying clover-leafs in the sky above the desert. Other times, we would go to Elephant Butte Lake and take pictures over it.

However, test missions are what I liked most, and we did a lot of them, like the following sequence, a GBU-27 bomb drop that was shot at 5-frames per second.

It was an honor and pleasure working with the Dragon Team, developing and expanding the capabilities of one of the most unique aircraft the world has ever seen.

5 COUNTER MEASURES

SILENT ATTACK WARNING SYSTEM (SAWS)

The Silent Attack Warning System (SAWS) concept evaluation program was developed to detect incoming missile threats to tactical aircraft. Three infrared sensors from different contractors were mounted on the rear panel of the 4950th Test Wing's C-141A tail-can aircraft.

Several phases of SAWS testing were conducted at White Sands. The first two phases utilized Chaparral surface-to-air missiles, and AIM-4G air-to-air missiles launched from F-4 aircraft at ground targets before airborne testing began.

During the third phase, the AIM-4G's were fired from F-15 fighters at the C-141A to see if sensors could detect the incoming threat.

The AIM-4G missiles minus their guidance systems were fired just out of effective range, while aircraft were precisely controlled by WSMR ground controllers using state-of-the-art monitoring systems.

The systems proved effective in determining that incoming threats flying behind aircraft could be detected using this technology.

SNOWSTORM

Snowstorm was another defensive countermeasures program that the Air Force was developing at the time for large cargo carrying aircraft such as the C-5 Galaxy. In this test, a C-5 would fly over the High Speed Test Track at Holloman AFB. At a determined point, track personnel would fire a rocket sled down the track to simulate a missile launch. The aircraft's infrared sensors would then detect the threat and dispense countermeasures automatically. This was the largest aircraft we ever used for testing. After the test was over, we caught up with "Fat Albert" and videotaped several minutes of it flying over White Sands.

ADVANCED STRATEGIC AND TACTICAL EXPENDABLE FLARE (ASTE)

Developed concurrently with Snowstorm, was the Advanced Strategic and Tactical Expendable (ASTE) flare, an infrared (IR) flare that fighter pilots could dispense when encountering an incoming missile threat.

As you can see, the QF-106 dispenses a burning flare that lights-up the sky, telling everyone where he is.

With an IR flare, you generate heat, but the flare's color is undetectable to the human eye, increasing an aerial platform's ability to survive in a tactical environment.

6 DRONES

82ND AERIAL TARGET SQUADRON (ATRS), DETACHMENT 1/DRONES

When I first arrived at Holloman, the 82nd Aerial Target Squadron was flying QF-100's. These were full-scale drones flown remotely from modified control vehicles. They were used as aerial targets for both surface-to-air and air-to-air missile tests. Within a few years, most of the QF-100's had been shot-down. Before being replaced by the QF-106, we flew a photo sortie documenting both aircraft over several WSMR sites.

Afterwards, I got a chance to fly in one. It's the only aircraft I ever flew that you felt a "kick" when you went into afterburner. As I kept pushing the control stick forward to maintain level flight, we just kept climbing in altitude. What a blast!

We also used QF-86's and subscale drones, the BQM-34 and the MQM-107. MQM-107's were used as targets, and towed targets, which we would chase. This made for some very interesting flights.

The pilots I flew with thought it was funny that I would guide them into position for target release, hold a split second, and tell them to go back quickly as the target deployed. It went something like this, "forward ... forward ... forward ... back, back, back, back."

Since the MQM-107 was remotely flown, the drone's pilot had no idea where we were, and flew wherever he wanted. Now add 300 feet of cable attached to the target, and hold on to your hat, in my case, camera. You were in for one helluva ride. It seems ridiculous, but the program managers wanted to see the deployment of the item, its flight characteristics, and retraction back into its carrier. This was all done ten feet away from the test item at speeds up to 250 knots. Pretty crazy!

SHOOTER, DRONE, AND CHASE

Part of the job of being safety chase, was to look over the shooter or surviving drone after the shot. This was to ensure everything on the aircraft looked normal, and no damage had occurred. If everything checked out, we'd call out that the aircraft was "clean and dry," meaning the aircraft was okay to continue the mission, or the drone could return to base.

7 TEST SUPPORT

586TH FLTS AT-38 GPS (GLOBAL POSITIONING SYSTEM) MISSION

As GPS came of age, our commander saw the potential how onboard systems could change our mission, and benefit everyone on WSMR. With GPS equipped T-38's, we could support both air-to-air and surface-to-air programs, flying profiles against air defense systems, such as Hawk, Chaparral, and Patriot, enabling operators to differentiate targets as friend of foe. We did this, and much, much more.

The two 586th Flight Test Squadron (FLTS) AT-38 aircraft in the above formation have flight engineers operating GPS data recorders. These units allowed the aircrew to navigate mission profiles to within one degree of accuracy, and record each pass for later analysis.

586TH FLTS HELMET CAM DEVELOPMENT

The idea for helmet-cam came from Lt. Col. Ken Hutchinson, my first commander at Holloman. One day, he commented that it would be nice if a pilot could document a mission from his or her perspective.

Afterwards, I contacted aeronautical engineers at Eglin AFB to see how long, and how much money it would take. They replied that it would take two years and $700,000.

Unfazed and having my Op's Officer approval, I set out to create the world's first helmet-cam video system certified for ejection seat aircraft. Using our group's resources, off-the-shelf components, and small team of experts, we fashioned a system through trial and error.

After a few ejections down the high-speed test track, certification was granted, giving the squadron unprecedented ability to do what no other flight test organization in the world could do, simultaneously acquire photographic coverage in three different formats from a single aircraft. It also lowered operational and support costs to our customers, and allowed us to document the entire mission from beginning to end.

Later development at Eglin AFB, allowed the system to be integrated with telemetry pods, so live video transmissions from the chase aircraft could be accomplished. This allowed test personnel on the ground to witness for the first time "live" what only a few got to witness in real-time. Not bad for a small group of people who had some ingenuity, time, and three-thousand dollars.

586TH FLTS AT-38 ECM (ELECTRONIC COUNTER MEASURES) POD

As with GPS, our commander recognized that if we utilized AT-38 airframes instead of T-38's, we would improve our carrying and g-load capacities. With a few modifications, our aircrews could fly and operate several types of electronic countermeasure (ECM) pods, confusing both air and ground based radar systems during tests. This conversion, along with GPS, and Helmet-Cam innovations changed our mission from test support into being a full-fledged Flight Test Squadron.

8 MISCELLANEOUS MISSIONS

FORWARD AFT RADAR TRACKING (FART)

The B-2 Stealth Bomber was built at a cost of 2 billion dollars each and needed the capability to fly into enemy territory, drop its payload, and return undetected. However, the first 5 prototypes had one problem, they could be detected by radar. Although the radar cross-section of the aircraft was small, it had to be eliminated.

In order to accomplish this, the B-2 had to be airborne, while its radar cross-section analyzed to find where the "hot spots" were coming from. To make this happen, Northrop Grumman and Hughes Aircraft joined forces to develop an airborne radar scattering laboratory that the bomber could fly between.

To see if the concept worked, two A-3 aircraft were modified and flown to Holloman to calibrate their systems against different types of aircraft, the AT-38 trainer, C-141 transport, and B-1B bomber. Once perfected, the aircraft would fly to Edwards AFB, and test the B-2 for flaws, allowing engineers to design modifications that would allow the bombers to carry out their wartime tasks.

On Northrop Grumman's A-3, modifications included a ten-foot fiberglass tail extension, adding what looked like a flying saucer that housed a radar antenna. This addition was needed to isolate the radar from the metallic structure of the aircraft. On top of the vertical stabilizer, a camera housing modification allowed operators to verify the alignment of aircraft flying behind them.

The plane was also outfitted with a radar calibrator that weighed 300 pounds that could be deployed 500 feet, and then retracted using a Kevlar cable.

On one mission, the cable snapped as the reflector came back to mate with its carriage, and fell to the ground. This reinforced the need that you always had to maintain situational awareness, and never assumed everything was going to go as planned.

Although this program created some of the most undesirable aircraft mod's imaginable, it worked, showing where the hotspots were. At the time however, I don't think the public knew how close the B-2 program came to being scrapped.

F-117 COLOR SCHEME SHOOT

Although I flew with the 57th Wing's, Dragon Team, I rarely got an opportunity to fly with the 7th, 8th, and 9th F-117 fighter squadrons. After eight months of trying, I finally got my chance. However, the Saturday before the flight, I was participating in a softball tournament. During one of the games, I was walking back to second base and stepped onto the bag. Unknown to me, the base wasn't properly secured and I severely twisted my ankle.

When I got home, I iced down and elevated my ankle hoping that the swelling would go down by Monday. By Sunday night, my ankle was still twice the size of my boot. I called my commander and asked what kind of physical shape I needed to be in to fly. He told me that I had to walk out to the plane with both boots on and climb into the aircraft. I then asked if I could just paint my foot black and hop in. He said no. So I had to wait for my ankle to heal.

Six months later, the 49th Fighter Wing wanted to paint their T-38 chase planes glossy black with silver lettering. In order to get Air Force Chief of Staff approval, they needed pictures showing how the paint scheme would look alongside the F-117. I now had my opportunity.

The F-117 landing shot looks quite mild. However, the pilot has to yaw the plane to the right to clear the canopy rail from my view, as I wedge my legs against the fuselage for balance.

The F-117 and T-38 in formation over Holloman was shot with the Wing Headquarters centered between them in the background. This picture was later used as a backdrop for Ben Rich's retirement in a hangar at Lockheed's famed Skunkworks.

Sometimes, the subject matter just present themselves to you. That's what happened when I looked above my canopy. Our aircraft were perfectly and proportionately stacked, so I took the shot.

Before the flight, the F-117 pilot had requested training support from an Air National Guard tanker unit. Usually, no refueling was ever sought during test missions. For me, it was just another opportunity to take pretty pictures.

One of my favorite shots was this F-117 over White Sands. My pilot was the 7th Fighter Squadron Commander. Although we had never flown together, we knew each other fairly well, since our families attended church and school together.

During the flight, we practiced chase techniques along the way. One technique was to roll over another aircraft, so I could take a picture that would look like it was on a flat plane. As you can see, he did it perfect, not only once, but twice. After the flight, he commented that this was one of the most strenuous flights he had ever flown. This was after thinking photo chase would be an easy task to do.

RE-ENLISTMENT CEREMONY

Re-Enlistment ceremonies are a long-held tradition in the military. Although many have been done in airlifters, not many have been accomplished in fighter or trainer type aircraft. The Dragon Team's Op's Officer asked me if I would do him a favor and document a ceremony taking place during flight for one of his enlisted personnel. One of the requirements for enlistment ceremonies is to have a flag as a backdrop, which you can see. Not only did this create a unique shot, but also a memorable event in the member's life, allowing her to serve four more years in the Air Force, while taking in the grandeur of White Sands Missile Range from above.

HOLLOMAN F-15'S

The four F-15's in echelon are A-models from Holloman AFB. They were the oldest F-15's being operated in the Air Force, and were due to be replaced by the F-117 Stealth Fighters that were stationed at Tonapah, Nevada.

Abiding by the military's decision to reduce forces after Operation Desert Storm, the Air Force deactivated all F-15A's while keeping F-15C and later models. Looking at the planes, there's very little difference visually between the A and C models, the main difference being in the plane's avionics and radar upgrades.

Prior to the F-22, the F-15 was the best air superiority fighter in the world, having both superb performance and flying qualities. A plane's flying quality is just the way it handles, whether or not it's in-synch with the human body. The F- 15 was the standard that all fighters were measured against, as was its predecessor, the F-86.

This occasion marked the final time the 49th Fighter Wing's F-15A's flagship aircraft would be photographed together in flight. It was late afternoon, and we were flying passes in front of Sierra Blanca, the highest peak in Southern New Mexico. We began a 180 degree turn to start a North to South run. The sun was quickly going down as I saw the shot developing. Although it's a spectacular shot, I hesitated for a moment, or two trying to decide if I should take it or not. Sometimes, what you think is a so-so shot, turns out to be one of the best pictures you'll ever take.

AIR SHOW

The pilots from Flight Systems Incorporated, a private contractor, asked one day, if I would mind flying with them in their F-100, which was scheduled to perform a two-ship flyby with an F-86 during the Wing's Open House. That was a no-brainer; I never gave up an opportunity to fly, especially in vintage aircraft. After we took-off, we loitered above the range for an hour before our slot came came-up. Not only did I have the opportunity to take pictures of the F-86, but was given the 100's stick for half-an-hour. What a joy to fly, nimble and easy to control. Then came our turn to perform, we had one pass, and one chance, to align the F-86 and the crowd below, and here it is.

LEAD-IN FIGHTER TRAINING (LIFT)

The Air Force lead-in fighter training program (LIFT) was conducted at the 479th Tactical Training Wing until the early 1990's when the Air Force decided students graduating from the AF Undergraduate Pilot Training (UPT) would learn fighter tactics at their new units of assignment.

Before that, all fighter pilots were trained at Holloman. To accommodate this workload, the Air Force stationed approximately 120 AT-38's on Holloman's flightline. This ocean of blue jets was affectionately known as "Smurf Jets" for their distinctive camouflage paint scheme of blue and gray.

As peripheral units associated with our squadron grew with Flight Test Engineers, agreements with the 479th and our squadron allowed non-rated crewmembers to fly with them on non-training missions.

Once they found out about our photographic capabilities, more flights became available for me that supported their requirements. At the end of one mission, I was able to form up four of the 'Smurf's' as they flew in finger-tip formation above Holloman's main gate.

9 POST MISSION

POST MISSION

Usually, we completed a test within fifteen to twenty minutes after take-off. After that, we would burn our fuel down to the aircraft's landing weight. We could accomplish this a variety of ways; going supersonic at low level, having mock dog fights, doing acrobatics, or practicing photographic techniques. Most of the time, we chose the latter. As we gained experience, nothing was off limits. It didn't matter what position we were in, we always got the shot.

SMOKING HOLES

If a drone was shot down, and we had time and fuel, we would go back to the impact area, and get a photo of the shooter aircraft above the smoking hole.

Examining the picture, it looks like there is nothing to it, but to get the shot, we needed to act fast, because the smoke and flames would dissipate quickly. To do this, the chase pilot would take over the flight lead immediately.

He would then direct both aircraft downwind from the crash site a few miles, turn around, line-up the sun angle, and let the photographer direct both planes into position to take the shot. It all happens very, very quickly.

LANDSCAPE DIVERSITY

Being in New Mexico, you wouldn't think you would have a diversity of backdrops at your doorstep. Vast areas of desolation separate the various landscapes that the Land of Enchantment is noted for. Flying high-performance jets puts a different twist into what "local" actually means. Within five to ten minutes of take-off, you can be over mountains, sand dunes, lava fields (Malpais), or large bodies of water. The landscapes are not only diverse, but are unique due to the clear and crisp New Mexican sky.

FB-111

This FB-111 was associated with GBU-28 testing, the bunker buster bomb designed to kill Saddam Hussein during the last hours of Desert Storm. This aircraft was assigned to Eglin Test as you can tell by the ET on the tail. It is flying over the North central section of WSMR known as, "The Malpais" or lava fields.

B-52H

A B-52H flies low level over sand dunes on WSMR. The deep shadows cast off to the side indicate its early morning or late afternoon. In this case, it's late afternoon. Notice the photographer has the sun to his back, allowing him to both model and gather large amounts of detail on this plane. The bomber was out on the range flying an AGM-143 Have Nap missile test.

F-15 AT 90 DEGREES

The pilot in the F-15 is banked at 90 degrees. Behind him is Salinas Peak. At 9,500 feet, it is the highest peak on White Sands. Flying approximately 100 feet away is the photographer in the chase plane. To accomplish the maneuver, the plane is rolled quickly, dropping below the chase aircraft.

If you look at the wings, you will notice the ailerons are displaced. The top ailerons are canted down and the bottom ailerons are canted up. This differentiates the lift, and allows the plane to roll rapidly allowing the photographer to capture it as it becomes perfectly vertical.

F-117 OVER ELEPHANT BUTTE LAKE

This knife-edge shot of the F-117 was taken over Elephant Butte Lake, approximately 70 miles west of Holloman AFB. From the side of the F-117, you can see there's not much to it. Although it is a huge plane, it looks small when viewed from the side. With the cockpit raised above the fuselage, pilots could see rather well out of it. Below the cockpit, are the grates that cover the engine inlets. You can also see the angles that were built into the fuselage. Both elements were crucial to the whole design.

F-15, QF-106, AND B-57 OVER DUNES

These overhead photographs of the F-15B, QF-106 and B-57 Canberra were all taken above the gypsum dunes of White Sands. To do this consistently, you have to think about the geometry involved. As you look out from the cockpit, it's impossible to see straight below. So what do you do? Cut a hole in the floor or shoot out the back. Remember, we only had training jets and fighter aircraft.

What you have to do, is find a procedure that allows the photographer enough canopy space to work through, while the pilot rotates the aircraft around an object you want to shoot. My pilot's would do this between 350 to 450 knots, while pulling 3-g's, as they maintained safe flight operations at the same time. As for me, I had to be 100 percent focused, since I would have less than a second to judge if I was correctly positioned or not.

To start the procedure, we began on the right side and adjacent to the aircraft we wanted to photograph. This always gave me enough room in the cockpit to operate. The pilot would then climb and perform a barrel roll over the plane, trying to maintain the same distance we started out with, keeping the aircraft below us centered as I shot through the canopy's side. What I was looking for was canopy alignment. If our canopy was further ahead, the aircraft's nose below us would appear pitched down. If it was a little behind, the nose would appear pitched up. Unless you had the canopy's exactly aligned, the perspective would be off.

The F-15 below, with rippled dunes beneath it, was the first over-the-top picture we shot after perfecting our technique. It took over a year-and-a-half of practice to analyze what needed to be done to get an aircraft to look like it was on a flat plane. Once perfected, we could apply the procedure to any aircraft we photographed, and get the same results.

Notice the dune patterns. They're all different sizes and shapes. We could control this by our altitude, direction, and time of day we flew.

The shot of the QF-106 is from directly above. It's a supersonic delta-wing interceptor that was built from 1957-58, and was capable of Mach 2 plus speeds. It never had true upgrades to its radar, and the system never garnered any weapons to speak of. Although it carried AIM-4 missiles and rockets, a gun could also be mounted inside its weapon's bay. The F-106's went out of the Air Force inventory in the early 80's, and were turned into drones.

The B-57 Canberra was a British designed bomber flown by numerous countries, including the United States. In fact, NASA had test versions with elongated wings and large turbofan engines that could fly up to 80,000 feet. The one pictured here, was a British test platform. It carried three crewmembers, a pilot up front and two others in back. For a thirty year old plane, it only had 3,000 flying hours on it, and was immaculate inside and out. Our squadron hosted their unit, while they flew laser tests with the Army. Although the British bomber crews were lots of fun, they weren't nearly as exciting as their fighter counterparts, which are probably the most enjoyable pilots you could ever be around.

TAIL-CAN C-141

This C-141 was one of the initial C-141 prototypes ever built, and is one of two C-141's A-models never converted into B-models during the late 1970's. The plane has always been a test platform and was operated by the 4950th Test Wing out of Wright Patterson AFB and later at Edwards AFB. The rear of the plane was modified with a large round cylinder, or "tail-can" that stuck out, allowing engineers to mount different types of test articles on the back. Below on the desert floor is the butterfly shaped Lake Lucero where gypsum crystals are formed that creates the White Sands.

F-100'S

Here is a unique picture of three F-100 Super Sabers in formation. They were flown by a contractor at Holloman and were part of an Army program. They operated there for several years. On this particular occasion, we had the chance to intercept their flight and get another pretty picture.

T-38'S OVER SIERRA BLANCA

The T-38's in fingertip formation over Sierra Blanca, New Mexico were unique to the Air Force, since they were painted black to match the F-117's. We always set-up these shots a few miles downwind to where we wanted to shoot, allowing us time to adjust the spacing, stacking, and background distance. Once in place, I would tweak the composition by telling my pilot to go up or down, or zoom in or out, since I always used normal focal-length lenses. Although the aircraft separation looks picture perfect, it's not the technique pilots are taught, and was awkward for them to fly.

F-15 HERO SHOT

This is an F-15 hero shot. I can't say it's just a hero shot, because it happens to be a hero shot of Lance Grace, my commander in the F-15 he used to fly at Holloman. Shooting someone's hero shot in an F-15 is trickier than you think. First, you need to know how much fuselage to shoot to make the composition look good. Then, the nose needs to point up slightly to give the plane an angular profile. If you don't, the wing looks flared-up, and the plane doesn't look masculine. Then, the chase pilot needs to adjust his elevation so you can compose the background with just enough air between the bottom of the aircraft and the ground. Finally, the pilot needs to look at you. That's the easiest part because there's only two things a pilot wants more than flying, a picture of himself, and a picture flying his plane.

SQUADRON COMMANDER

F-86 JOY RIDE

My favorite photo, on a special flight, was this F-86 hero shot with the canopy retracted. In 1962, when I was ten years old, my family was on a road trip in Southern Illinois when we passed by Chanute AFB located in Rantoul, Illinois. As we came into town, sitting off to the right of the road in a little memorial was an F-86, the air superiority fighter of the Korean War. I'm not sure whether I really knew what it was called back then. All I knew was that I had this little plastic model at home that could shoot little rockets off the wings.

That was 1962. In 1995, I got the opportunity to fly a real F-86, and it was a beautiful thing. If you look at the picture, behind the oxygen mask is a big grin on my face. I'm cruising along at 215 knots with the canopy back, and my hand on the canopy rail.

GR-1 TORNADOS/JAGUARS

After Desert Storm, the British brought their Jaguars and modified ground attack GR-1 Tornadoes to Holloman to conduct flare tests over White Sands Missile Range. Flares are used as infrared decoys. The idea is, an infrared tracker, either on the ground, or in the air can lock onto an aircraft (such as a heat seeking missile). By dispensing flares, the missile could momentarily break track from the aircraft and switch to the decoy.

Trying to follow the decoy, the missile eliminates itself by going stupid, taking the aircraft out of harm's way. With this mindset, all kinds of unique flares can be uploaded on the aircraft. The Brit's spent about a month at Holloman, and were absolutely a joy to have on base.

GERMAN AIR FORCE

The planes in the above formation happen to be German F-4's. The German Luftwaffe has trained their pilots in the United States since 1955. The German Air Force flew out of Luke AFB originally, then moved to George AFB during the late 1970's, and then to Holloman in the 1990's.

When they came to Holloman, they were flying modified F-4 fighters, which made them a formidable plane, though their performance wasn't as comparable to our F-15's and 16's. Even worse were the high operational and maintenance costs. However, the F-4 was definitely a type of aircraft that was very close to my heart.

—Lieutenant Colonel Lance "Amazin" Grace, Ret.

F-18 C

Periodically, the Navy would fly F-18's to White Sands to test fire AMRAAM missiles.

The F-18 is flown by both the U.S. Navy and Marine Corps. It is also flown by other countries, such as Spain and Finland. The F-18 is a fly-by-wire jet originally designed by Northrop Corporation to compete against the F-16. At the time, it was called the YF-17, and lost to the F-16 during the fly-off competition.

After the competition, McDonnell Douglas got hold of it, turned things around, and named it the F-18. McDonnell Douglas then combined forces with Northrop to build the F-18 for the Navy, since the Navy didn't like single engine fighters, such as the F-16. A single engine fighter has basic inherent problems, especially in the combat role operating off a carrier deck.

If an aircraft experiences engine failure after take-off, you don't want to disrupt carrier operations. Aircraft cycle times are absolutely crucial from take-off to landing, almost to the minute. Aircraft are going to land closely to what they had projected prior to take-off.

If flight times become out of synch, the rest of the planes that are flying have to follow, screwing up the entire operation, so you cannot allow this to happen. The minute you take-off and have engine problems, operations aren't going to be willing to recover the aircraft right away. They are going to want the pilot to stay in the cycle. That's why the Navy has planes with multiple engines, so they can continue flying normal op's while in-flight emergencies take place.

F-4 W/ECM POD

This is an F-4 with an ECM pod attached to it. ECM stands for electronic counter-measures. The pod is designed to "play around" with radar tracking devices by using different techniques, such as varying velocity and range gates. Being strapped to the seat with little or no wiggle room, you really had to twist to get a shot during high-g turns. After flights like this, you would have bruises and burst blood vessels, and wondered where you got them from.

THE AIRBORNE SEEKER EVALUATION TEST SYSTEM (ASETS) C-130A

This specially modified C-130A carried the Airborne Seeker Evaluation Test System (ASETS), and operated out of Eglin AFB. If you look under the forward fuselage, you can see that a turret has been mounted. The turret moves up and down and can be internally stowed for take-offs and landings. Once airborne, the aircrew can lower it, allowing it to test a variety of sensors and seekers for long durations.

F-111'S

On the left are two F-111's flying in formation, one from Eglin AFB, Florida, and the other from Cannon AFB, New Mexico. The nearest one carries an AQM-131 ECM pod which was standard for the fleet. The F-111 had a long and twisted history, a nightmarish folly designed back in the 1960's as the plane that would do everything. The legacy it leaves is; you cannot design an aircraft that does everything, period!

FLIGHT SYSTEMS INCORPORATED (FSI) F-86

This aircraft was used for flight test support and gunnery missions over WSMR. It would carry twenty-foot tow darts and fly them over the range for gunnery practice. At the correct altitude, the pilot would deploy the dart by releasing 2,000 feet of cable, and fly S-maneuvers as planes came from behind and shot at the darts. During the early 90's, this practice slowly disappeared as newer methods developed. When the F-15's left Holloman, the tow dart disappeared with it.

F-15 GOING STRAIGHT UP/DOWN

There is nothing like climbing than going vertical in fighters. The coolest part, is watching the digital altimeter spin as you gain altitude. It wasn't until the F-15, F-16, and F-18 that you could light-up the blowers and climb like a bat out of hell.

Shots like this require that you have equally performing aircraft. Pilots fly an inside loop while in formation. When you get to the loop's outer edge, the aircraft should be perfectly vertical if only for a second. That's when you take the shot. The hardest part is judging the background during that instant, the horizon needs to be horizontal, or it wasn't done correctly.

However, what goes up has to come down. Whether you have engines spooled up or pulled back, speed brakes in or out, you come down extremely fast. It is something you simply cannot do in "heavy" aircraft.

KNOWING YOUR CANOPY

The biggest friend or foe an aerial photographer has is the canopy that he or she shoots through. Knowing where scratches or smudges are that cannot be removed is the responsibility of the photographer. The military is not going to replace it just because it has small imperfections, so you learn to shoot around them.

Along the same principle, not all canopies are created equal. The F-15 canopy is large and hard to get your lens up too. This makes it difficult to eliminate reflections. Also, canopy points located every 45 degrees are distortion free. These are your effective shooting areas. Everywhere else is distorted.

The F-16 canopy is smaller and more bulbous. As with the F-15, points located every 45 degrees are distortion free. However, the effective shooting area is only six to eight inches wide. The tightness of the cockpit and canopy makes it difficult for photographers to operate in, especially if you're tall.

The compromise is the T-38. It has a near distortion free canopy except in the recesses of their curves. The cockpit has enough room to operate in, while allowing you to place the lens up to the canopy, allowing reflections to be eliminated.

These images were captured while flying in the T-38. This F-15 was shot while both aircraft performed S-turns. During the maneuvers, the aircraft closed in enough for me to take the shot over my shoulder.

The descending F-16C was shot looking forward and to the side. No other jets I know of would have allowed me to do that. For my money, the T-38 is the best photo chase plane on the planet.

PEOPLE ASK, WHY DID I DO IT?

In publications, aerial photographers often explain why or how they do their job. The only thing I know, is either you have a passion for it or not. If you do, you take precautions against what may keep you from succeeding. This allows you to totally focus on the job at hand.

For me, it meant using dark cloths that covered instrument panels, and taping areas where black paint had chipped off. You wore gloves, used subdued colored helmets, removed colored patches, used black painted cameras, and taped over chrome lenses, eliminating your number one threat, canopy reflection. If you did this correctly, the picture looks like there was nothing between you, and the aircraft being photographed.

This also required placing the camera lens as close to the canopy as possible without scratching it, while struggling with harnesses that held you tightly in place. Your arms ache as your plane goes through positive and negative g's, holding onto cameras that vary between 0 and 160 pounds as events start to unfold.

That's just the aircraft portion. On the ground, pre-planning and coordination were discussed during numerous briefings, allowing all participants to be on the same page. Cameras and lenses needed to be clean and lubricated, film properly loaded, and batteries fully charged and cameras tested. I looked at the camera as a tool, an extension of my body that could capture moments in time. I couldn't waste efforts on the mechanics of operation. It had to be automatic. I didn't have second chances with multi-million dollar projects on-the-line.

Flight test is the only job I know that tests your intelligence and physical capabilities on the edge of the flight envelope. It gives you one chance to succeed, while risking everything. It is great when you can defy these odds, and do it daily. Only a few ever get to experience this feeling, and makes you appreciate living life to the fullest.

MISSION COMPLETE-RTB (RETURN TO BASE)

Most sorties last an hour. Your body is tired and your flight suit is soaked with perspiration.

You want to take-off your oxygen mask that's been glued to your face, open the canopy, and let the fresh air in. You un-strap the seat belts as you taxi back, allowing you to move around and get blood circulating in your butt again. But you feel great. All your cameras have worked, knowing you got all the shots you required. All you think about now, is going back up, and doing it all over again

PLANES AND SPECIFICATIONS

B-52 STRATOFORTRESS
Length: 160 feet 11 inches
Wingspan: 185 feet
Height: 40 feet 8 inches
Max Speed: 650 mph
Max Takeoff Weight: 505,000lbs
Range: 8,806 miles

B-57 CANBERRA
Length: 65 feet 6 inches
Wingspan: 64 feet
Height: 15 feet 8 inches
Max Speed: 580 mph
Max Takeoff Weight: 55,000lbs
Range: 3,380 miles

A-3 SKYWARRIOR
Length: 76 feet 4 inches
Wingspan: 72 feet 6 inches
Height: 22 feet 9.5 inches
Max Speed: 610 mph
Max Takeoff Weight: 82,000lbs
Range: 2,100 miles

QF-86 SABRE
Length: 37 feet
Wingspan: 37 feet
Height: 14 feet
Max Speed: 687 mph
Max Takeoff Weight: 17,000lbs
Range: 1,000 miles

F117A NIGHTHAWK
Length: 65 feet 11 inches
Wingspan: 43 feet 4 inches
Height: 12 feet 5 inches
Max Speed: 656 mph
Max Takeoff Weight: 52,200lbs
Range: 765 miles

C-130 HERCULES
Length: 97 feet 9 inches
Wingspan: 132 feet 6 inches
Height: 38 feet 8 inches
Max Speed: 345 mph
Max Takeoff Weight: 155,000lbs
Range: 2,047 miles

C-141 STARLIFTER
Length: 168 feet 4 inches
Wingspan: 160 feet
Height: 39 feet 7 inches
Max Speed: 563 mph
Max Takeoff Weight: 343,000lbs
Range: 2,500 miles

AT-38 TALON
Length: 46 feet 4.5 inches
Wingspan: 25 feet 3 inches
Height: 12 feet 10.5 inches
Max Speed: 858 mph
Max Takeoff Weight: 12,093lbs
Range: 1,090 miles

A-6 INTRUDER
Length: 54 feet 8 inches
Wingspan: 53 feet
Height: 16 feet 2 inches
Max Speed: 643 mph
Max Takeoff Weight: 61,620lbs
Range: 3,245 miles

C-5 GALAXY
Length: 247 feet 10 inches
Wingspan: 222 feet 9 inches
Height: 65 feet
Max Speed: 570 mph
Max Takeoff Weight: 840,000lbs
Range: 7,272 miles

F-100 SUPER SABRE
Length: 50 feet
Wingspan: 38 feet 9 inches
Height: 15 feet 4 inches
Max Speed: 848 mph
Max Takeoff Weight: 35,600lbs
Range: 1,733 miles

FB-111 AARDVARK
Length: 75 feet 5 inches
Wingspan: 63 feet
Height: 17 feet 2 inches
Max Speed: 1,616 mph
Max Takeoff Weight: 100,002lbs
Range: 2,925 miles

QF-106 DELTA DART
Length: 70 feet 8.8 inches
Wingspan: 38 feet 3.5 inches
Height: 20 feet 3.3 inches
Max Speed: 1,525 mph
Max Takeoff Weight: 41,831lbs
Range: 1,500 miles

BRITISH JAGUAR
Length: 55 feet 2.5 inches
Wingspan: 28 feet 6 inches
Height: 16 feet .5 inches
Max Speed: 1,056 mph
Max Takeoff Weight: 34,610lbs
Range: 875 miles

F-4 PHANTOM II
Length: 63 feet
Wingspan: 38 feet 3 inches
Height: 15 feet 5 inches
Max Speed: 1,583 mph
Max Takeoff Weight: 61,652lbs
Range: 1,750 miles

F-8 CRUSADER
Length: 54 feet 6 inches
Wingspan: 35 feet 2 inches
Height: 15 feet 9 inches
Max Speed: 1,135 mph
Max Takeoff Weight: 34,000lbs
Range: 1,425 miles

F-15 EAGLE
Length: 63 feet 9 inches
Wingspan: 42 feet 10 inches
Height: 18 feet 6 inches
Max Speed: 1,665 mph
Max Takeoff Weight: 68,000lbs
Range: 2,762 miles

BRITISH TORNADO
Length: 54 feet 10.5 inches
Wingspan: 45 feet 6 inches
Height: 19 feet 6.25 inches
Max Speed: 1,453 mph
Max Takeoff Weight: 61,620lbs
Range: 2,417 miles

F/A-18 HORNET
Length: 56 feet
Wingspan: 40 feet 5 inches
Height: 15 feet 3 inches
Max Speed: 1,190 mph
Max Takeoff Weight: 51,900lbs
Range: 1,379 miles

F-16 FIGHTING FALCON
Length: 49 feet 4 inches
Wingspan: 32 feet 8 inches
Height: 16 feet 8 inches
Max Speed: 1,500 mph
Max Takeoff Weight: 48,000lbs
Range: 2,002 miles

KC-135 STRATOTANKER
Length: 136 feet 3 inches
Wingspan: 130 feet 1 inch
Height: 41 feet 8 inches
Max Speed: 600 mph
Max Takeoff Weight: 322,500lbs
Range: 11,015 miles

DC-X DELTA CLIPPER
Height: 39 feet
Diameter: 13 feet
Max Weight: 41,700lbs
Max Thrust: 13,000lbs

ABOUT THE AUTHORS

Michael Williams is a retired Senior Master Sergeant, and former Flight Test Photographer who spent ten and a half years of a twenty-six year Air Force career in Flight Test.

From 1989 to 1995, he was assigned to the 586th Flight Test Squadron at Holloman AFB, NM, a one-deep position supporting all Department of Defense weapons testing over the White Sands Missile Range.

Accumulating 883 hours in the air, he was qualified in 28 types of aircraft, operating still, video, and motion picture cameras that spun-up to 2000 frames per second.

During this period, he participated in the top Department of Defense test programs that supported OPERATION DESERT STORM, and further developed GPS, stealth, and defensive electronic countermeasure technologies, along with optical and radar guided, hypersonic, and heat seeking missiles for bomber and fighter aircraft, including the advanced tactical and multi-role fighters, the F-22 Raptor and F-35 Lightning.

To document tests, his camera of choice was a one-off, 70mm sequential still camera from Photosonics, capable of 20 frames per second, bore-sighted (attached and sighted) to a high-speed motion picture camera that ran up to 200 frames per second. Under normal conditions, the unit weighed 23 pounds, but under 7-g's, its weight increased accordingly.

Besides direct test support, Sergeant Williams's images informed Congress and Air Force hierarchy of the latest developments in weapon system technology. His imagery also appeared in aerospace advertisements and periodicals, and was honored by a second place finish in the 1995 Aviation Week and Space Technology's International Photo Contest.

However, none of these images would have been possible without the dedicated and skilled pilots that he had the privilege to fly with.

Lance Grace, is a former Command and Test Pilot, flying over 4500 hours in more than 50 types of aircraft. After graduating from the Air Force Academy in 1975, he completed pilot training, and was assigned T-38 Talon instructor pilot duties at Arizona's Williams AFB. Later, he served two operational tours flying F-4E Phantom II's while in Germany and North Carolina.

In 1985, Lance attended the Air Force Test Pilot School (TPS). As a test pilot, he began flying operational test missions at Edwards AFB in F-4 and A-7 aircraft, then flew F-15 Eagles as a member of the F-15 Combined Test

Force. During the summer of 1989, he was assigned instructor pilot duties at TPS, but within weeks, was unexpectedly transferred to Holloman AFB in New Mexico where he would spend the next six years, the longest tour of his Air Force career. During this time, Lance would fly test missions in F-15 and F-16 fighters, and test support missions in T-38 and AT-38 aircraft.

When Lance arrived at Holloman in the fall of 1989, dramatic changes were about to happen. The Berlin Wall began to fall, the Soviet Union broke-up, and the Cold War ended, resulting in dramatic force reductions in the US military. Two years later, Desert Storm began, ended, and was followed by more force reductions. Every military organization was trying to justify its existence or reinvent itself. As a satellite organization under the 46th Test Wing at Eglin AFB, Florida, high level support for the squadron's mission in New Mexico was mostly non-existent even though test engineers and pilots from the wing continuously came to Holloman to fly missions over the White Sands Missile Range.

Being the 6586th Test Support Squadron Operations Officer, he realized the potential that the White Sands Missile Range and squadron offered to other military services and National Security. A year later, he was selected as the youngest commander for an active flying squadron, becoming the Commander of the newly formed 586th Flight Test Squadron, but the celebration was short lived as the squadron lost most of its operational funds, and more than 80 percent of its personnel due to budget cuts as the test mission began to flourish.

Needing to broaden the mission and operate more efficiently, Lance acquired and modified two AT-38 aircraft for test support missions, and operated them as the only unfunded flying aircraft in the Air Force, charging fees for service. At the same time, he radically changed the organizational mind-set by doing more with less. He hand-picked key new members, gave them multiple responsibilities, and supported them in their quests to continuously figure-out quick and economic ways to successfully accomplish the mission. The pace accelerated to the point, where in his last year, he and his Operations Officer, David "Doc" Nelson, flew more flight test missions than anyone else in Material Command, including all the test pilots at Eglin combined.